Down 'long weth we

An anthology of
Cornish dialect stories

Compiled by James Whinray

Tor Mark Press · Redruth

THE TOR MARK SERIES
FOLKLORE

- Classic Cornish ghost stories
- Classic Devon ghost stories
- Classic West Country ghost stories
- Cornish fairies
- Cornish folklore
- Cornish legends
- Customs and superstitions from Cornish folklore
- Demons, ghosts and spectres in Cornish folklore
- Devonshire customs and superstitions
- Devonshire legends
- Down 'long weth we
- The pixy book
- Strange tales of the Cornish Coast

OTHER TITLES

- Charlestown
- China clay
- Classic Cornish anecdotes
- Cornish fishing industry
- Cornish mining – at surface
- Cornish mining – underground
- Cornish mining industry
- Cornish recipes
- Cornish saints
- Cornish smuggling industry
- Cornwall in camera
- Cornwall's early lifeboats
- Cornwall's engine houses
- Cornwall's railways
- Devonshire jokes and stories
- Do you know Cornwall?
- Exploring Cornwall with your car
- Harry Carter – Cornish smuggler
- Houses, castles and gardens in Cornwall
- Introducing Cornwall
- King Arthur – man or myth?
- Lost ports of Cornwall
- Old Cornwall – in pictures
- The pasty book
- Shipwrecks around Land's End
- Shipwrecks around the Lizard
- Shipwrecks around Mounts Bay
- Shipwrecks – Falmouth to Looe
- The story of Cornwall
- The story of the Cornish language
- The story of St Ives
- The story of Truro Cathedral
- Tales of the Cornish fishermen
- Tales of the Cornish miners
- Tales of the Cornish smugglers
- Tales of the Cornish wreckers
- Twelve walks on the Lizard

First published 1997 by Tor Mark Press
United Downs Industrial Estate, St Day, Redruth, Cornwall, TR16 5HY
© Tor Mark Press 1997
ISBN 0 85025 359 4

Cover artwork by Beryl Sanders

Printed in Great Britain by Burstwick Print and Publicity Services, Hull

Introduction

Cornwall in the late eighteenth century was at the forefront of the Industrial Revolution, yet in other ways it remained utterly remote. Cornish miners in particular had no contact with English ways, and this continued to be so until the spread of railways and of compulsory schooling in the second half of Queen Victoria's reign.

This isolation allowed a flourishing and expressive dialect to be preserved, along with distinct habits of thought, quite untainted by formal education. The gentry and other educated Cornishmen could see the inevitability of change, and some set out to record the dialect before it became diluted. Some chose verse, perhaps influenced by Burns or the Dorset dialect poet William Barnes: later writers tended towards prose.

Each writer emphasized different aspects of the dialect by using their own 'phonetic' spelling. It may seem strange at first, but if you persevere, and listen to the sound, it will soon become familiar. Some of the differences in spelling represent regional variations. At a time when a man might never go more than twenty miles from home in his whole life, there was no uniformity of pronunciation even within Cornwall; it is after all over eighty miles from the Tamar to Land's End. In the east, you would hear the 'z' substituted for 's' which is characteristic of Devon and Zumerset; at St Ives, but nowhere else, words such as bay and ray were pronounced 'baa' and 'raa'.

The dialect has its own perfectly consistent grammar and vocabulary: Chaucer's contemporaries would have found many aspects of both quite familiar! A phrase such as 'cudn blaw nor strick' uses blow and strike in archaic meanings (breathe and move) which survived only in Cornwall. The pronunciation of 'thought' and 'daughter' as 'thoft' and 'dafter' was also once widespread, strange as it may sound now. On the other hand a phrase such as 'cheeld vean' contains a word from the Celtic language of old Cornwall, and 'clunky' is pure Norse.

We have provided a brief glossary, but suggest you don't get bogged down by looking up every word. Indeed it is a very selective glossary, concentrating on words essential to an understanding of the stories.

Our hope is that the pieces will be interesting and entertaining in their own right, and that you will enjoy their vigour of expression. 'Tedn defficult 'toal, my dears!

Charms

I one day hinted to Tom Moyle that I did not believe in charms, to which he replied, 'That's all because you are a doctor and want to sell your medicine, but I tell ee what et es Maister, charms es no good wethout faith, but weth faith they'll cure more'n you can weth your baistly ould physic. Why, I cud tell ee scores and hunderds of cures by charms.

'Now when I was a young man, I worked to a bal weth a man caal'd Jack Tregoning, and he suffered from a toothache nuff to kill a hoss; he tried everything a'most but twas all to no good. At laast he got that bad he cudn' chow nor cudn' clunky, and got to look thin and wisht. Well, just then he heerd of an ould wumman what cud charm, and so he went to her, and she gove un something wrapped up in a whit clath, and towld un to tie et on to es right arm and never taake et off day nor night, and Jack ded et and never had toothache arterwards.'

'But what do you suppose was wrapped up in the cloth, Tom?' I asked.

'Well, I never thoft anybody wud ax that question,' replied Tom. '"Tedn' what I do spoase, 'tes what I do knaw, and as Jack es dead now I'll tell ee how I do knaw.

'Jack was a braave quiet chap when he was sober, but when he was in drink he was allus tremenjous cross. Well, waun faist day he had a drap

too much and got quar'lsum, and then the boys taised un and that maade un wuss, so he tookt off hes coat, turned up hes shirt sleeves, thrawed hes hat 'pon the ground, and said to um, "Come on anybody, I'll fight or wrastle ory man in England, and theer's my hat. Who'll pick un up?"

'But nobody dedn' pick un up, 'cause they dedn' want to fight weth a drunk man, but the booays begin'd to kick tha hat about and maade a football of un. Than Jack got maazed and chaased tha booays, and catched hes foot 'pon a stoane and faall'd down flop, and theer he lied. Well, I seed tha cloth tied on to hes arm, and I felt curus like, so I said to tha booays, "Lev'n alooane to me, he's my cumraade, I'll taake caare of un." So when they was gone, I tookt off tha cloth and found a tooad's head theer, all dried up like. So I tied un on agen to hes arm and keept et a saicret, 'caase doan't ee see, ef Jack knawed what was theer the charm wud be brok, and the toothache wud cum back agen.

'But Lor' bless ee Sir, that's nothing to some charms I've knawed. Why, there was ould Jan Patt, he was a powerful charmer, and was a local praichur too; he used to charm by prayer and suplificaation. When I was a booay, home weth we, faather had a stubbut apple tree that used to bear braave large apples, but somehow he faalled off bearing and got covered all ovver weth a lot of ould fossil stuff. The Parson said twas caalled likeun, but I cudn' see twas like anything in perticklrer, so I axed a gardener and he said it was caalled litchun, and he advised faather to have the tree pruned; so when winter was come, twas done. Well, jist then we had two little pigs died, and faather burried um onder the apple tree for luck.

'Well, waun day ould Jan Patt com'd round, and we axed un to charm the tree, and he ded so. P'raps you might not b'lieve et, but that year we had a better crop than ever we had afore.

'Jan wud never be paid for hes work, 'cause he used to say twould break the charm, but he wodn' agin having a present sent to hes house, so faather sent un a g'eat big laarge basket-full of apples, and Jan was plaised sure nuff.

'The most wonderfullest caase I ever knawed though, was that about Billy Treglown, and I knawed he from a cheeld. Billy's faather's proper name was Willyam, but he was allus caalled Billy for short and he dedn' like et. Well he was a shoemaker, and when his booay was born the naybours all said, of course you'll call tha cheeld arter your awn naame, but Willyam said, "I shaan't do nothin' of tha soort, 'cause ef I do he's sure to be caaled Billy. I've maade my mind to give tha cheeld a scriptur naame."

'So he sarched the Bible all through a'most, and in the Book of Job he found what he thoft a very proper naame for the son of a shoemaaker, and that was Bildad the Shuhite, and christened Bildad the cheeld was; but twodn' no good, for he was allus caalled Billy from that, so theer was ould Billy and young Billy.

Well, young Billy grawed up a braave stuggy booay, and fat, and when he was ould enough to go to work, hes faather said to un, thee cussn't be a miner 'cause thee'rt too fat to clem the ladders – thee must be a shoemaker. But young Billy cudn' do much to that traade; he was so fat he cudn' clukey down very well, and settin' 'pon a stool all day long was mor'n he cud stummick.

So at laast he got bad, and the doctor said he was lemphatic, which I s'pose do mean too much fat about hes lembs, so the doctor gov'n a bottle of traade to taake, but that was no good. Then he gov'n powders and they was no better. And then he gov'n pills, and aw, my dear, they pills nearly kill'd un; they broft un down so law he cudn' blaw nor strik, and hes clooas hanged 'bout un in larrups, and he looked so wisht everybody thoft he was goin' into a recline. At laast, ould Billy said hes booay shudn' taake no moore of tha gashly stuff, but he wud have un charmed, so he tookt off to Zacky Treloar.

'Zacky was what they do caall a whit witch, and knawed everything a'most. He used to keep yarbs, and roots, and charms, and all soarts of things hanging 'bout the house, and when he seed young Billy looking so wisht and flabby, and when ould Billy told un what the doctor said, he loff'd sure nuff. "Lemphatic may be a very good naame for a fat booay," said Zacky, "but I can tell ee what's the matter weth un, he've got the lurgy," and he towld Billy he must give up shoemaking and work in the fields, and sweat at et, and he gov'n a charm to wear round hes neck.

'Well, next day Billy went digging taaties, and he towld hes faather in the evening he cud feel the fat working off hes lembs, and he knawed the charm was acting, and then hes faather got a plaace for un 'pon a farm.

'Now at that farm there was a maid of all work caalled Keranappuc Polglaze, and she had such a temper they nick-named her Spitfire. When she was in her tantrums everybody knawed et and cleared off, all ceps Billy, and he faaled in love weth her, and arter a time they got married and lived in a little house 'pon the plaace; but theer wodn' much happiness 'cause theer wodn' no cheldrun.

'So Billy went waunce moore to Zacky and towld un es grief, and axed un to charm hes wife, and he towld Billy that she must waalk round the house nine times, and say this varse:

Alpha beta little booay
And grammur delta blaw:
Epsilon Zaytur eta theaytur,
Iota kap a lamb you knaw!'

'Where did Zacky get that verse from?' I asked. 'I b'lieve he got et from a skulemaaster,' was Tom's reply. 'Zacky says tes Greek and I s'poase tes, for I caan't maake much sense in et, but tes wonderful powerful in charms. Well, when she had done that, she was to set 'pon a three-legged stool for a full hour wethout spaikin' a word, and she ded et too, for she was a strong-minded young wumman, but she said twas the biggest trial she ever had in her life.

'Well, then the charm begin to act, and a wonderful chaange tookt plaace, for she had nineteen cheldurn in sixteen years. Moast of um was booays, and g'eat strappin' chaps they are oal of um, like g'eat ellum trees, but they all got their mother's temper.'

'But Tom,' I said, 'you are wrong in your chronology; you have allowed your imagination to get the better of your discretion. I can't see how she could have had nineteen.'

'And you caall yourself a doctor, do ee,' said Tom, interrupting me, 'why, caan't ee se she had three paair of twins?'

'And what is become of these strapping chaps?' I asked. 'Well, Sir, moast of um es gone abroad – waun went to 'Merrica, another to New York, and another to Caliphonia, and the rest is scattered 'bout waun plaace and another. I caan't zackly say wheere they are! Billy es still alive and as fat as ever, but what weth being charmed and having a scoldin' wife, and faather of a laarge family, he've nevver had no time to git the lurgy sence he was a booay.'

I saw that Tom was getting tired, so I offered him a pipe of tobacco, and having loaded myself we sat smoking together in silence for a few minutes. At last he said, 'I knaw you doctors doan't like charms. Now theer was Dan'l Deeble, he used to suffer from ...' Looking at my watch I found I was half-an-hour late in calling on a patient, so I apologised to Tom, and told him I would see him at some future time to hear the story of Dan'l, and as I walked away, I heard him chuckling to himself, 'Haw, haw, haw, I knawed he cudn' stand charms!'

A weighty ghost story

Waant a story do'ee boys? (said Jan Jacobs, what keept tha kiddleywink ovver to Wendron Church Town, Jacob's Ladder they caaal'd un, 'caase he wor that tall). Well, I'll tell 'ee a ghost story thes time, what I never tould 'ee afoar.

Waunce 'pon a time a ould man an' es wife, caal'd Jan and Mally Datsun, keept a lettel shop – for smaal thengs, shuggar, trikle, tay, snoff an' bacca, an' sechlike traade, ovver to Cross Lane End; 'twor a wisht coose soort o' plaace, an' peepul dedn't keer fur to go by 'pon night time, 'cause o' tha fower ways mitten, an' ould Tom Kissel, what killed himself an' wor buried theer; a loansum an' shevery spot 'twor, shure nuff. Well, they lev'd by theerselfs, leastways an ould fella caal'd Tim Temberleg slaipt theer fur company, like. He hadn't got but waun leg, laiv'd t'other en Truraw Infirmary, an' comed out weth a wooden waun, an' a skrooch!

Waun night they wor oal to bed, an' nigh 'pon mednight theer com'd a orful racket; fust long, a crash, an' nex, a smash, a bang, an' then a grone.

Jan wor slaipin', an' thoft 'twor Mally weth tha spassums, an' wend en her stummic – but 'twadn't. Then they caal'd to Tim en nex chaamber – 'Ded 'ee hear summit?'

'Aw,' groaned Tim, 'we be oal dead men, Jan, you, an' me, an' Mally! Dead copses we be, an' no mistake!'

Mally wor rollin' 'pon her bed like a porpus 'pon dry land, when 'pon a suddent they heerd, drip, drop, drip, drop, like summit 'gain ovver steers. Fust long, Jan thoft 'twor laiks from tha datch. But, aw, my dear, 'twor wuss than that! Jan strick'd a light weth tha tendur box, an' maade es knukels blud sum coose, he ded.

Jus' then Mally gov'd a skreetch – 'Aw, Jan, what es ut? 'Tes theer en tha corndur! 'tes theer! shut to un, my dear! shut to un! 'tes zackly like Aunt Tammy Daw, what hang'd harself long weth hur stay laace, over to Sandybottom.' Jan seed a long figgur en whit weth summit 'pon es head, in tha corndur, an' catch'd up Tim's wooden leg, an' drash'd un 'gen tha objec', an' down he went flop 'pon the planchen, an' they never seed nort but a puff o' wend, an' a orful smell o' brenstone. 'Twor a straange theng en my 'pinion – but that dedn't 'count for tha crash, an' tha grones.

Well, artur mite a while, they insulted togethur, an' 'greed to go ovver steers, an' see what wor theer. Mally cudn't put herself ento hur cloas no ways, she wor propurly bewattled, she wor. Laast o' all she com'd out

'pon the planchen long weth hur bedgownd an' rud petticoat, Jan's fustin jackut, an' a ould black bunnet on tha top of hur head. She clapp'd hur feet ento hur pattens, catch'd up hur ould umbreller, an' went cleck, clack, ovver steers. Jan com'd artur, an' when he put foot 'pon the laast steer, holler'd out, 'Aw, Molly, theer's Murdur! theer's Murdur! theer's gaate ould pools o' blud! I be farely stagg'd en ut, I be!'

Mally an' Tim com'd foar, an' theer wor blud, an' no mistaake! What wor to be don'd? Mally (wumman like) wor fust to find mouth-speech, an' she said – 'We wadn't but dree o'us laast night, Jan, an' we be dree o'us now. Praise tha Loard for tha saame.' (For Mally, you must knaw, wor a perfessor ovver to Bethal Chapul, an' Maister Bangum, the praichur, all'ays praised Missis Datsun's hoam-maade wine, an' craim an' trickle.) 'So narry waun of us baan't dead nor murdered – Provedens have ben fine an' good to we, Jan, we might hav ben oal dead an' berrid en tha symetary, we might! I thenk, f'roal, we shud sarch fur tha dead body, fur theer mus be waun somewheers!'

Artur that device o' Mally's, Tim took up dree brath basons, an' a chaamber brush – Mally catch'd up two box hetters an' her ould green umbreller – an' Jan trapes'd artur, weth tha butt end of a ould gun, what hadn't got no barrel to un, an' they went foar like a flock o' geese altogethur, waun arter t'other, but cudn't see nort, nor hear nort, 'cept 'twor their own hearts thumpin' 'gen their cloas, an' then, 'pon suddent, a graate ould owl beginn'd to hoot, an' that farely maade um quail, 'way long weth fright. Artur that, Jan said, 'Mally, my dear, a lettul cumfort wud be good now, ef ever 'twor!'

'Aw, iss, Jan, I awnly wish Maistur Bangum wor heer, how bootiful he wud emprove tha ocashun, as he do caal ut! I bleeve he'd soon lay thease heer sperets, he wud.'

'Hould yer paice, Mally, do 'ee, doan't ee taalk so waik! Old Bangum wud lay tha sperets en es awn stummic, an' no mistake! A sarm-sengin' ould 'umbug, that's what he es; sopeing ovver waik faymails, an' aitin' an' drenkin' theer 'usband's craim an' trikel, an' curran wine. Bangum's no more en my eyes than a flay en Saint Pitter's Church!'

'Hoosh, Jan, hoosh! You'm nort but a carnal man, an' very dark, I be feer'd!'

'Never mind, Mally, doan't ee lev us tongue-fite thease heer wisht times. Tim, ould man, what's tha clock, do ee knaw?'

'Nigh 'pon haaf artur waun, I shud say, consederin' oal we've seed, an' heerd, sence tha clock strik'd twelve, an' we wor oal skeer'd! Shall I go an' see, Jan?'

'Iss, do ee, Tim,' says Mally, 'you aant got but waun leg an' yer skrootch, an' me an' Jan have got fower, so you waan't stap en tha muck, an' blud, saame as we shud – lev us knaw tha time, do ee.'

Way clops Tim, ovver tha temberin' hill, an' when he held up tha candel to tha faace o' tha clock, he cried out, 'Hollo, what's heer? Why, clock's runn'd down rite to twelve o'clock.' He then open'd tha caase doar, an' skreeched out, 'Why Mally, 'tes tha wights, they'm oal goan! that's what tha row wor, clock's down an' wights es down! an' they'm oal bluddin'! Theer's pools o' blud en tha clock caase – these es rum an' no mestaake!'

Mally, 'pon hearing thes, faall'd bak en hur cheer like a man shut to, an' tossin' 'bout hur arms like a wendmill, drash'd off her pattuns and skreech'd out, '"Tedn't rum, Tim, 'tedn't rum, 'tes my bes RUD CURRAN' WINE! – 'tes my best RUD CORGUL – maade 'gen Chrismus!'

Then Mally took to sterricks – sum violent they wor – loffin' waun minnut, an cryin' nex – farely zoundin' 'way, she wor, an' shoutin' out – 'Murdur! Theeves! Bugglars! Sperets! – we be oal dead we be!'

Artur a bit she got moar decomposed, an' tould Jan she put sex bottuls o' curran' wine ento tha clock caase for 'ticlar frens (Iss, iss, thoft Jan, 'ticlar frens – Maister Bangum an' sichee wauns I rekkon) an' tha wights had fall'd an nack'd um oal to scats an' jowds.

Luke Martin's Cowld

Some people, when they do prent a buck, do say when they do begin that they doan't do et for nothin' else in the world but for other people's good, and that ef awnly waun man es maade better by raiding of et they're happy, they are.

Now I arn't like that theere. What I do say es this: ef anybody who got a cowld do find out how to cure un by raiding of this heere, I arn't too proud to be paid for et. My name es Luke Martin and I do live out to Blackwaater, and they may send me so many postage stamps as they mind to. The best of it es, everybody do knaw me, and everybody do knaw that what I do say es rail facts. So fur as I do knaw, et edn't much matter how you do catch cowld, but the way I catched my cowld was this. I was a blacksmith waunce, I was (I arn't now, mind) and the shop wheere I worked to catched fire. Trying to put out that theere fire, I catched my cowld, and lost my vooice and the puttiest set of tools that ever you seed. Et dedn't matter much 'bout the vooice, but 'twas a wisht thing to lose they tools. Well, the fust thing, I beginned to sneeze.

Aw, my dear, how I did sneeze. So somebody says to me, 'Why, thee'st got a cowld, Luke. Go and put they feet in hot waater and go to bed.' So I ded. I hadn't ben theere long when a man comed in and said, says he, 'Thee wust never git well like that; git up, and wash thyself all ovver in cowld waater.' So I ded. Then in comed another and he said, 'You must feed a cowld and starve a faiver.' So I ait so much as ever I cud stuff for the cowld, and then dedn't ait nothin' for hours and hours for the faiver. I do love to do things fitty, I do. So when the aiting time for the cowld comd, I went to a cook's shop what had jist ben opened by a straanyer, and paid what he axed for me to ait so much as I mind to. When I'd a-done, he said, 'Do people down heere often have cowlds, do they?' 'Iss, blaw,' says I. The next time I went to that theere shop, the shutters wor up, and he wor gone.

As I was goin' hum, I seed Sam Moyle, and he told me that ef I wud awnly clunk a quaart of hot saalt waater, the cowld wud be got ruds of. I tried et. Sick? says you. Narry a shag that ever lived wass haaf so sick as I wor. Hot saalt waater may be good for some cowlds, but not for my cowld. I was a braave strong man, I wor. I cud wrastle weth arry man in the parish, but the traade I tuk maade me so waik as a cheeld. I caan't tell ee now oal the things I ded taake. There was cowld porter and shuggar; hot porter and shuggar; gin and trikle; rum and honey; organ broth;

elder tay; and harby tay of oal soorts. 'Twas no good; my cowld, ef any deff'rence, was wuss.

Waun thing I tuk did aise me for the nounce, and that was a pint of gin and onions every twelve hours. But aw, my dear, my breath got that bad, nobody cudn't stop en the same room weth me. At last, waun chap says, 'You waan't get no better hum heere, you must try chaange of air.' Well, I ded. I went ovver to St Ann's, and went out to say, and went 'pon top of the Bikkin, and when I wor up theere, I seed a wumman, and spok to her; and when she heerd I wor hoase, she towld me to put 'pon my chest a laarge mustard plaaster when I went to bed; and I ded. But et dedn't do me no good, for my comraade what slaipt weth me waaked up in the night a-hungered, an' ait every bit of un, clath an' all.

And I went to chapel, and aw, my dear, you shud have heerd me sing baass then. The man what played the baass-vile was so vexed as fire, you cudn't heear he. When I towld un 'twas awnly a cowld I had, he said, 'Aw, that's all right. I wudn' be no good ef you was to stop heere weth a vooice like that.'

Well, I got wuss and wuss, and, thinks I, I waan't stop heere among straanyers, I'll go back hum. Chaange of air waan't cure me, I knaw. When I got back, 'twas the saame ould littan from everybody I mit. 'What a wisht man,' says waun. 'Thee'rt so poor as a craane,' says another. 'Why, Luke, thee'rt nothin' but a shadda,' says another. And so they keept on.

At laast a wumman that had ben in a Infirmary in Lunnon said that they cured cowlds theere by rowling a man up in cowld wet claths. I was so bad that, thoft I, I caan't be no wuss, so I'll try et. And I ded try et. But never no moore, my dear, never no moore will I do that, live or die. 'Twas a bitter cowld night and they stripped my back and brist oal naaked, and then wrapped yaards upon yaards of cowld wet claths oal round me, tell I was like Moases's britches, no shaape nor form. I thoft 'twas oal ovver weth me then, I ded. I cudn't blaw nor strick, nor I cudn't clunky. So I tored off the gashly things, and never took nothin' and never ded nothin' no moore to cure that cowld.

And then I got better, and I've had lots of cowlds sence that, but never waun so bad. The things I tuk might do some people good, and so they may try em if they mind to. Ef the wust ded come to the wust, it cud but kill 'em.

A tale of witchcraft

I s'poase you nevver knaw'd th'ould Decky Poddle, ded ee? That wadn' es propur naame like a theng, fur ee wor chressen'd Rechat Rundle, ee wor, but they allus caal'd un Decky Poddle, caase why, ee wor stiddy shovin' es nawse en awther peepul's bizness! Aw my dear! ee wor sum deep ould chap, he wor. Ee'd got a clain-off way of smoothin' ennyboddy ovver, I can tell ee, an' ee'd do et that grand that ee'd feerly haale your chack-teeth out an' you wudn' knaw et! Howsomedever, th'ould Decky had a-got sum offul bad strakes en un, iss my dear! Ee wor allus shimshankin' 'bout the parrish, ee wor, peckin' up awl the scandal ee cud fang, an' what wor a naashin' sight wuss than thes, ee wor 'so laazy as Lawrance', iss ee wor! Hurd wurk an' Decky faal'd out 'eers agone! Why, ee wudn' taake a stiddy job 'pon noa'count! Ee wor fancical of chaanges, ee wor, fur I heer'd un say ovver an' ovver 'gen that 'a chaange of wurk wor good as a titch-pipe!'

Now laaziness, you knaw, edn' wuth nothin' onless tes well follied, an' th'ould Decky steck'd to et like a man, iss ee ded, tell laast of awl ee shet ento a braave aisy billet sure 'nuff, where ee hadn' got nothin' to do ceps watch the waater-stampses down to Polgooth Valley. Awl the 'eer round, wentur an' summer, Decky wor night coor, so ee'd got awl the day long to geekey 'bout an' peck up tha noos, an' ee'd a-got awl the night droo fur to chow et ovver like a theng!

How Dicky Poddle caught the dandy dog

Now, ee hadn' ben a-watchin' they theer stampin' mills purtecklar long afore ee beginn'd to see an' hear tha moast desmal thengs sure nuff! Wan bootiful moonlight night, soas, while Decky wor a-lyin' down en tha Lodge an' tryin' fur to catch a nod, ee heer'd what ee thoft wor tha blast of a huntin' horn, so up ee got an' ren'd out ov doors to waunce, when, Lor, massy me! ee seed tha lettle peeple, iss, ee ded! Theer they wor an' noa mistaake, weth a clain-off pack ov dandy dogs, yappin' an' gain' like good wans – an' theer wor tha Peskies, iss my dear! deck'd off en rud jackets, whit britches an' top-boots, ridin' 'pon little hosses noa higher than your hand – an' theer wor tha huntsman a-blawin' ov tha horn sum lesty!

Decky wor like a man bewattled moast – ee cudn' blaw nur strick – but ee seed um, iss ee ded, an' as wan ov tha dandy-dogs wor a-crossin' ov tha floors, wat ded th'ould Decky do but clap a g'aate ould keeve clain down ovver un!

'Whirraw, Whirraw!' ses Decky, 'I've got ee saafe 'nuff now!'

But aw, my dear! ee'd no soonder ben 'an said et than that theer dandy dog shet clain out droo tha bung-hole, an' Decky losed un arter awl! 'Aw dear, aw dear!' ses Decky, 'Thes es a wisht poor job, thes es! Ef I'd awnly catch'd thicky theer dandy dog, I'd hav car'd un roun' tha country en a shaw. I'd have charg'd a penny a head dismisshun fur to see un, an' I'll wadge I shud hav maade a clain-off levin', iss, wethout workin'! Aw dear, aw dear, I've ben an' lost a fortin', that's sartin sure, that es!'

Now arter this heer deventure, theer wadn' a night scarce but wat Decky seed or heerd sum gashly theng or nuther! A dog wethout a head wud be stiddy rennin' awl ovver tha plaace – g'aate bools av fire wud be glaancin' awl aroun' un – an' witches, ridin' 'pon theer broomstecks wud be chitterin' sum offul! Then the machinery begin'd fur to go awl wrong – tha stampses wud be stiddy knackin' out – tha graates wud be allus breakin' – so that poor ould Decky cudn' have a mennit's paice fur awl tha night. Aw, my deer, ee wor en sum wisht way 'bout et, I tell ee, an' 'twadn' very long afore ee cum'd to tha delushon that ee wor bewattled!

'I'll wadge,' ses ee, 'that thes heer carry on es tha wurk of Un Jinny Hooper! I allus thoft she wor a witch, an' now I be sartin sure ov et.'

Aunt Jenny and her fiercesome familiars

Well, Un Jinny, you must knaw, wor a fine queer lettle ould wumman long weth a braave-size charley 'tween hur shoulders. She wor moast naashin' dark grained, iss she wor – tha sken ov hur wor so 'brown as a Toney' moast – tha g'aate rowlin' eyes ov hur wor so big as braave size saucers like a theng – an' the weight of hur wor wan hundred an wan pound zackly! Aw my dear! ef you do lev so long as Tantrum Bobus you waan't nevver see anawther wumman like she noa moar!

She wor a witch right nuff, she wor, an' thees heer is how she got the power to wurk hur witchery. She used fur to kaip two lerrickin' g'aate ould toads onder tha hearth-stone – they wor wat she used fur to caal her 'familiars', they wor, an' thes es how she maade em obadiant to hur will: she fed em long weth consecrated bread! Aw, my dear! they wor sum fierce, they wor! Why, Lor' massy me! they'd jump to ennyboddy en a mennit, iss they wud, an' they'd whep out theer g'aate long tongues sum gashly, I can tell ee! Every boddy most 'bout wor feer'd ov Un Jinny an hur toads! So Decky feel'd sartin sure that 'twor Un Jinny wat had ben an' ill-wished un, an' ee pitched fur to reckon hur up an' fur to romance ovver hur to a purty rate, iss ee ded.

Well, soas, 'twadn very long arter thes afore ee had to suffer a moast tremnjus lost sure nuff! Ee'd got a black dunky, ee had, caal'd Boxer, wat ee used fur to sot purtecklar vally 'pon, an' wan Munday mornin' as ee wor cummin' hum from wurk, ee found the poor ould Boxer lyin' dead jist outside the town-plaace! Decky wor propurly fatch'd down awl to waance, iss ee wor!

'Poor ould dunky,' ses ee, 'me an' you wor jist like brethers, we wor, an' now I've ben an' lost ee! Aw dear, aw dear! I shaan't hear thy bootiful baas voice noa moar, I shaan't! Un Jinny's witchcraft hav a-ben an' pearted us! Howsomedever, I doan't wish hur no hurt, but, ef 'twor so plaisin', I shud like a ridgement ov dunkeys fur to keck hur fur ever an' ever! I doan't knaw what to do, or whichy coose to steer, n't I! I be a hart-brokken man, I be, an' ef I doan't hav a drap ov summut fur to kaip my sperrits up, I shall be gain' an' committin' susanside, iss I shall!'

The pub runs dry

So off Decky went to have a drap of cumfort. Ee entered tha village kidleywenk an' caal'd fur a quaart ov hum-brew'd. The landlord took'd up a mug, put un under tha tap an' turned tha kay – but aw, my dear, tha beer wudn' run!

'Hullo,' ses Bunnyfaace, 'thes es a naashin' queer job, thes es! Tha barrel edn' out fur I awnly pitch'd un issterday. I reckon tes a bit of hop got ento tha tap.' Weth that, ee stoopied down an' blaw'd up tha mouth ov un, but aw my dear! ee cudn' git noa beer to ren! 'Well,' ses ee, 'I'll try tha awther barrel. An' so ee ded, but 'twor zackly same long weth that wan too! Ed cudn' git noa beer to ren 'tawl! Jist then anawther chap waalk'd up an' knack'd fur a pint ov beer. The lanloard took'd down a smaal mug, turn'd tha tap, an' straange to say, tha beer begin'd to ren awlright fur ee!

'Queck, landloard, queck!' ses Decky, 'Here, hitch my quaart, do ee, an' full un up now that tha beer's rennin'!' So Bunnyfaace took'd Decky's quaart, but ee'd no sooner put un under tha tap than, aw, my dear! tha beer stopped rennin' awl to waance! 'Darn ee,' ses Decky, 'Un Jenny's bewattled tha beer barrel, that's what's tha matter! that's plain nuff, that es! Tha beer'll ren fur ennybody else, but she waan't laive et run for me! I be en a purty stank I be, fur I caan't aiven git a drap ov beer! Semmin' to me, I be zackly like tha ould Blythey, allus en tha wuss plaace. Howsomedever, I waan't stop heer noa longer, but I'll go right hum an' bury up tha poor ould dunky!'

So away ee went, sinkt a pit, draw'd Boxer ento un, an' fore ee sturt to fulley en agen, ee ses, ses ee, 'Goodbye, Boxer. I s'poase I shaan't nevver see'ee noa moar en thus wurld, but nevver mind, you do laive a good chara'ter behind ee, an' you be better off'n I be, fur now Un Jinny waan't be able fur to bewattle ee noa moar!' Arter thes heer Fooneral Sarmon like a theng, ee fullied en the graave – went hum, fadgied out a tember toomstone, an 'described thes eppytaff 'pon un:

> BERRIED HERE LIES POOR OULD BOXER!
> AWL ES EARTHLY GRIEFS ES O'ER!
> EE WOR KELL'D BY JINNY'S WITCHCRAFT,
> MAY THE 2ND '34

That wor a wisht day for Decky Poddle, that wor! Ee cudn' feel aisy, do what he wud, an' when ee started off to work that ebenin', ee wor most 'bout out ov hart, iss ee wor! Ee dedn't knaw how, nur ee cudn' tell why, but ee wor feelin' zackly as ef sum offul theng wor 'bout to happen! Well, ee raich'd the bal, took't a walk round, an' seed that evverytheng wor gain' on braave an' keenly ways. Then ee went ento tha Lodge, lighted es pipe, and stratch'd isself out on the caffenter's bench, intendin', ef 'twor so plaisin', fur to catch a nod; but ee noa sooner begin'd to get cumberful like, than ee wor took'd sum bad weth tha wunders en es fengers an es toes! Thes heer wor awnly tha beginnin' ov es trubbles, understand. Tha arter claps wor a naashin' sight wuss than thes! Awl to-waunce ee heerd tha Peskies grezzlin' feerly as ef they wor teckled – ee heerd tha witches chitterin' like a flock of magpies as they went skittin' round 'pon theer broom-stecks! Then awl 'pon a suddent, tha stamps stood still!

Out Decky ren'd to see wat wor tha matter when, Lor' massy me, theer wor tha wheels standin' idle, an' tha waater gain' ovver em en a proper bowse! 'Good Lor',' says Decky, 'thes heer's a marracle an' no mistaake! Un Jinny's bewattled tha waater-wheels now, that's sartin sure, that es! Aw dear, aw dear, ef I caan't stop thes heer witch-craft, I shall be fooaced to laive tha country, iss I shall. I've ben an' loosed my dunky, I caan't git a drap ov beer, tha stamps es allus knackin' out, tha graates es stiddy breakin' – an' now the waater wheels waan't move! Whatever shall I do? Ef I caan't overcome Un Jinny's witchcraft, I shaan't hav no paice, that's sartin sure! Now that I thenk 'pon et, I've heerd um say, 'a spaade bitch to catch a witch!' Iss, I'll have wan, cost me wat she may.'

Dicky buys a spayed bitch ...

So nex' mornin' Decky sot off to look for a 'spaade bitch'. Many and many a long mile ee had to traapse, but at laaste, my dear, ee managed fur to git one, iss ee ded! Lor' massy me! Ee wor sum sot up ovver 'es bargain, Decky wor. Wheerever he went, ee used fur to laid hur 'bout long weth un, an' peepul wud be stiddy joakin' ov un, an' singin' out to un, 'Taake care, Decky, or Un Jinny'll have 'ee!' 'I doan't care nawthin' for Un Jinny!' ses ee, 'she caan't hurt me, she caan't! I do defy the Devil an' awl Un Jinny's witchery now that I've a-got a spaade bitch.' Then, my dear, ee'd pat hur 'pon the head sum luvvin' and whesker to hur like: 'Spaade bitch, catch tha witch! Ren, Jinny, ren!'

Well, for waiks an' waiks arter thes, thengs went on braave an' quiet ways. Ee dedn' see nur heer noa moar peskies nur witches; tha waater wheels wurked off awl right; tha stampses dedn' knack out 'tawl, and tha graates stopp'd breakin'. 'Whirraw,' ses Decky, I'm happy glad I boft that bitch, fur, sence I had she, Un Jinny 'an't ben able fur to do noa furder mischeef! I've broked tha spell, that's sartin sure, that es, an' Un Jinny's power es propurly den'd fur. Whirraw, whirraw!'

... and then two heifers at Roche Fair

Now, 'twadn' very long arter thes that Decky Poddle went to Roche Feer, weth the detenshun of buyin' a cupple of cows, ef so be as how ee cud awnly suit isself. Ee went an' lukkied round a braavish spur, ee ded, an' 'laast ee seed two cows, wat ee reckoned wud fit un proper sure nuff. Wan wor a lettle splatty yaffer, an' tha awther wor a proper lettle Blackfaace.

'Well, Meastur,' ses Decky, 'wat be axin' now fur thicky splatty yaffer an' thicky Blackfaace?'

'Do ee waant to buy?' ses ee.

'Coose I do,' ses Decky, 'or I shudn'ax ee!'

'Well,' ses tha farmer, 'as you be a braave lookin' chap now, you shall hav'em both for nineteen suvverins.'

'Shaan't gev ee that for em, 'tawl!' ses Decky.

'Wat will ee gev, then?' ses ee.

'Doan't like to be buyer an' seller too, I doan't,' ses Decky, 'so wat's your lowest fur em?'

'I waan't taake nawthin' less'n eighteen poun' ten!' ses ee.

'I'll gev ee eighteen pound,' ses Decky.

'Cum now,' ses the farmer, 'splet tha deff'runce, an' gev me eighteen poun' five!'

'Awlright,' ses Decky, 'I'll gev'ee eighteen poun' an' I'll kaip the five shellin' fur luck!'

'Dear, dear!' ses tha farmer, 'you be a naashin' tight chap fur a bargain you be! Howsumdever, I s'poase I must laive ee hav'em!'

'That's clain off, that es!' ses Decky. So ee whep'd out es canvas bag, plunk'd down tha eighteen suvverins, an' soon got en coose to sturt es humward journey.

Now 'tedn't a purtecklar aisy job to drive two yaffers, I can tell ee, but 'time an' pashence'll wear out moor stoane posses', an' at laast, arter a braavish sight ov trubble, ee broft um hum an' turned um out ento tha back meddaw fur tha night.

Aw, my deer! ee wor propurly lurged, Decky wor, an' insteed ov gittin' up eerly nex' mornin', ee lied en bed sum laate. Well, while ee wor slaipin' off sum swait, an' snoring braave an' hearty like a theng, es Mistess went out to have a look at tha noo cows, an' when she wor cum'd to tha meddaw wheere they wor, she got ento a purty towse, sure nuff! Lor, massy me! theer wor tha lettle Blackfaace cow a-gallopin' roun' an' roun', fur awl tha wurld like a hoss en a whem!

Frightened out ov hur senses 'moast, Mistiss Poddle ren'd off hum, glaanc'd up ovver steers, and singied out to Decky, 'Cumest out to waance you, fur tha lettle Blackfaace es a coosin' ov her tail! Un Jinny hav bewattled hur, that's sartin sure that es!'

An early case of mad cow disease

'Git long weth ee!' said Decky, 'you be allus seein' dubble, you be, but awl tha saame I'll go an' see hur fur meself!' Weth that, ee jumped out ovver tha bed, got ento es cloas sum queck, glaanced down tha tember hill, an' when ee cum'd to tha back meddaw, tha cows wor right nuff. Theer they wor a-lyin' down an' chowin' ov theer cud sum purty.

'You've ben an' maade a missment for waance, ould wumman!' ses Decky. 'I knawed you had! two bootiful bastes, now, baan't em,' ses he.

'Iss, they be two propur pecturs!' ses she. 'I tell ee,' ses he, 'Un Jinny aint a-got noa power ovver me nur minse, now that I've boft a spaade bitch. I do defy she an' awl her witchery!' Arter thes remark ee walkied off, went in, an' sturt to do a few keddlin' lettle jobs en the front garden.

Now, ee hadn' ben theer verry long afore ee heerd es Mistiss, scritchin' like a whitneck: 'Decky, Decky, where be to? Cum to waance, now, do ee! Tha cows es took'd!' Aw, my dear, he wor off like a skainer, iss ee wor, an' soon as ever ee com'd to tha field gaate, ee seed fur isself, iss ee ded! Theer wor tha splatty yaffer, an' theer wor tha lettle Blackfaace, gallopin' roun' an roun', feerly like a pair ov purlygigs! Iss, my dear, they wor a-gain' that coose, that sumtimes theer heads wor fust, an' sumtimes theer tails wor fust, an' twor a naashin' hurd job to tell t'awther from which. Decky tried awl evver ee knawed fur to stop em, iss ee ded, but Lor' massy me! Ee might so well hav tried to stop tha drivin' wheel of a fire

inyun! Well, soas, they theer cows keep'd on like thes heere, purlin' roun' an' roun' like a sheep weth tha whirls awl droo tha arternoon! Scores an' scores ov peepul com'd to see um, an' zackly as tha sun went down tha splatty yaffer an' tha lettle Blackfaace boath fall'd along an' died tha very saame mennit.

When Decky seed that they wor dead sure nuff, ee wor feerly like a maaz'd man, iss ee wor. 'I'll go right hum,' ses ee, 'fatch the spaade bitch to waance, an' then I'll go an' faace Un Jinny Hooper.'

Ee raich'd es cottage, went out ento tha back staable wheere ee allus kaip'd tha bitch, an' theer she wor, dead as a door nail, long weth hur drot cut!

'Aw dear!' ses Decky, 'I can see et now, iss I can! Un Jinny murder'd tha bitch fust, an' that wor tha way she managed to bewattle tha cows! Howsumdever, I'll hav magic for she, iss I will! I'll traapse right off to Plemmuth this verry night an' ensult tha White Witch 'bout et.' Weth thes detenshun ee ondertook'd tha journey, en due coose caall'd 'pon tha Witch, towld hur es misfortins, an' axed hur fur to help un. Well, she order'd un to go stright hum, taake out tha hearts frum tha two dead yaffers, steck um feerly full of fuss preckles, begin to rooast em for tha fire a lettle before mednight; an' while tha hearts wor rooastin', ee or she wat had bewattled un would be sartin to waalk ento es house. Well, soas, Decky went right hum agen, an' ded zackly as tha White Witch towld un.

Ee opened tha bullocks, took'd theer hearts out, steck'd um full ov fuss preckles, an' pitch'd to rooast um 'fore tha kitchen fire.

Now, zackly as tha clock strick'd twelve, Un Jinny Hooper hobbled en, cum'd up to wheere Decky an' es Mistiss wor settin', an' hobbled out agen wethout gevin' enny mouth-spaich 'tawl. Aw my dear, Decky wor en a proper boil ov sweat sure nuff, an' Decky's Mistiss zounded right away, she ded, an' lied 'pon the floor as steff as a bat! Nex' mornin', soas, tha noos wor awl ovver tha plaace 'moast, that Un Jinny had ben took't suddent, an' 'twor keenly nuff that she'd maake a die ov et! Howsumdever, she got ovver that awl right, but yet f'raal a moast tarrible jidgement faall'd 'pon hur famly 'fore the year wor our! Hur husban' waalk'd, onknowin', ento a mine shaft an' wor drownded, hur only son wor blaw'd to leck and jowds when shuttin' a hawl onderground, an' Jinny hurself took't to hur bed an' maade a mooast awful bad end sure nuff!

My Deventures to Faisten Time

by Jeremiah Penwarden

Plaise sure my dears, I'm feeling so paale as a cuddle, and so waik as a haaf starved cat. I haben got the maisles, nor the plumbaga, nor the rotabaga, nor the brown titus nor the green titus. No, tedn' that 'toal, but 'tes all awin' to Faisten Time. I doan't main the wild baist shaw into Trurraw, there's baistes 'nough to be seed wethout payin' a shellen to see um.

No, my dears, what I'm goin' to ascribe to ee es my deventures to our awn little faist. I must 'splain to ee that down 'long weth we, we do have a faist riglar wance a 'ear, and 'tes always the fust Sunday arter the morraw 'pon Christmas Day. Tha's the day my dears, when you do pay the rent ef you've got any money to pay un weth. Ef you haben and caant borrey, aw my dear, you're in a pretty stank sure 'nough.

But howsomedever, 'tes the Faist an' my deventures what I'm goin' to spaik 'bout. I must 'splain to 'ee that most av the Faist home along weth we es the day arter, an' then 'tes rabbit pie an' pudding, an' buyin' ginger bread nuts for your sweethearts, an' walkin' up an' down arm in arm, an' being devited out to have a dish o' tay weth all your first cousins, het settery, het settery. Ef I'd a done that my dears, there wouldn't ha bin no deventures to tell. But I like a git stoopid, I missed my way like, an' a wisht pore I've had sure 'nough weth my owld woman Betsy Jaane.

'Twas like this. I meet a nowld friend, an' he says, says he, 'Jeremiah, me owld dear, 'tes Faisten Time.'

'You're right,' says I, 'iss sure, coos tes.'

Says he, 'A Faisten Time we do belong to have a bit av a flaare-up.'

'You're right,' says I, 'iss sure, a coos, a coos.'

Says he, 'Ef you'll trait me to a couple of pints, Jeremiah I'll trait thee to a quaart.'

'I'm gaame,' says I, an' in we went. The landlord, a bra' civil man 'nough, was very perlite, he always es, 'specially when you've got money in your pocket. But I arn't a-goin' to say nothin' agin he, cause he dedn't fooace us in; we went in zactly saame as ef we liked hes beer, and dedn't want no foochin'. I drinked my cumraade's quaart an' he drinked my two pints, an' then we had a drap a gin to taake the frost out av our stummicks, an' then we had a pint or two more beer to cool our throtts, an' then some toddy, an' then some more beer, an' arter that I lost count, till I heeard the landlord say, 'Now me sons, plaise to git out, for 'tes shuttin' up time.'

I was a braave long time afore I could find the door, but at laast I got out an' maade for hum. Whether 'twas a earthquaake or no, I caant say, but the ground comed up three or fower times an' bumped agin' my nawse afore I got to our fore door, an' looked into the faitures of my owld woman, Betsy Jaane.

I 'spected a bit of a swogger, but she dedn't say nothin', but laided me in an' tookt off my hat, an' said, 'Now Jeremiah, me dear, lie down 'pon the mat afore the fire, till you've rested a bit.'

I thought to meself, 'The owld dear is braave and sweet, sure 'nough, iss she es,' but afore I could continny my deflections, I tumbled down 'pon the planshin an' faalled aslaip. What a passel a things do happen when we're slaipen', my dears. Why, any night you might be dreamin' av aitin' rashers av bacon an' smackin' your lips ovver it, while all the time the pig is gettin' chucked weth a gait turmut out in the crowe!

A grave awakening

'Massy me,' says I when I waaked, 'where am I?' For there, close to me 'pon the planshin', was a coffin, an' my fust cousin, Tommy Penwarden, was lyin' in un, weth a faace so white as a mellerd, and so long a'moast as a baase-viol.

'Where are ee?' says he, 'why, Jerry me booay, thee'rt dead – so dead as a worm what have a bin stanked 'pon.'

'Are I?' says I, 'tha's a wisht poor job then. How long have I bin dead?'

'Three days,' says he.

'I bluv thee'rt a liard,' says I, 'for semmen to me tedn' long sence I falled aslaip 'pon this here mat.'

'Why your whiskers an' heear es moast all gone a'ready,' says he. 'Feel um yourself, ef you doan't believe me.' So me dears, I put up me hand and I gove a screech that could be heerd a mile away ef your ears was long enough, for would ee believe it, my heear was cut short zackly saame as ef I'd jist comed out of Bodmint jail, an' as for my whiskers, well I had a putty paair wance, as Betsy Jane towld me when I went coortin' fust, but now me poor owld ching was zackly like a scrubbin' brush.

'Aw dear, aw dear,' says I, 'what ever shall I do? How long have you bin here?' says I to Tommy, who was all the time glaazin at me out of the coffin like a sticked pig.

'Three weeks,' says he.

'Three weeks,' says I, 'an' gone so wisht lookin' a'ready! Why, I shall never be aable to stand it.'

Then I feelt all chacked weth thust an' I says, 'I hop, Tommy, you waant tak et amiss, an' waan't tell tha Cappen av tha plaace 'bout it, but as you've ben heere longer 'n me, cust a tell you where I can git a drap av somefin to drink?'

'Drink!' says he, 'drink! You'll be a passel thustier afore you've a-done.'

'Then,' says I, 'I shall be frizzled up to a natomy, for I'm so dry as a chip now.'

Then I tried to git up, but somebody had fastened the mat round my legs, an' as I jumped up I gave a lurch to leward, an' went slap agin our kitchen dresser, an' away went Betsy Jaane's best taypot – a cloamin wan – an' knacked to bits; an' a yalla dish what we do have tappy-occa puddin' a Sundays in, he went arter un; an' three of Betsy Jaane's Granny's best cups and saucers; an' a cloamin image of Napoleon Boneypark, Emperor of Turkey or some such plaace; an' a plate or two an' four or five glasses. The scrash wor awful sure 'nough, 'an frighted our ould tom cat so as he gove a yowl, an' jumped clain through a quarry of glass, an' as I was trying to saave myself, I catch'd howld of the clock, an' the rusty ould nail comed out, an' he faal'd an' scat in hes faace, an' hes insides haben never bin wuth nothin' sence.

Afore I could pick up the sherds in runn'd Betsy Jaane weth the big broom, an' gove me a scat 'longside the head as maade me poor owld teeth rattle in me gums.

'You old vellan,' says she, 'you aren't content weth comin' home basely drunk, but you've a-brok all my chany to bits, iss you have. I'll knock the owld head av tha off, iss I will. That taypot, what my aant Joanna gove me, an' Granny's cups and saucers what I've tookt such delight in, an' dusted every Saturday, an' washed wance a month rigler, an' wance exter to Faisten time, an' thee've a-brok un, thee, thee...!'

I got vexed 'pon this, an' says I, 'Dosn't tha thee me.'

Says she, 'You ould rascal, I'll thee tha, and I'll thou tha, iss I will,' an' she haived to me agen weth tha broom.

'Aw, my dear Betsy Jaane, don't ee do it,' says I, 'doan't ee. I'm a dead man a'ready, an' to ha' ma brains scat out arter that, es more'n human natur can bear.'

'Dead, are ee?' says she, an' she gove me a gashly ould laugh, 'dead are ee? Then I'll bring tha to life agin putty quick, iss I will,' an' then down comed the gait brush 'pon my back this time, an' out she runned to the backlet an' brought in a pail of cowld soapy waater an' drashed it oal ovver me. So I up an' done no other but I screeched 'Murder!' so hard as I could, for I thoft Betsy Jaane, what promised to love an' to cherish me, 'll be the dath av me.

'Tedn cherishin', my dears, to scat a basely ould broom ovver your nuddick, an' to thraw cowld soapy waater down the back av your nek, aw no, that edn no lovin' an' cherishin' 'toal.

Well, when I screeched 'Murder!' somebody oppened the door and axed, 'Es there anything the matter?' You wudn't believe that a wumman cud be so decaitful, but afore I could spaik, Betsy Jaane says, says she, as ef butter cudn't milt in her mouth,

'Aw no, my dear, 'tes awnly Jeremiah have a-got the toothache tarrable bad,' an' she slammed the door again. 'Now Jeremiah,' says Betsy Jaane, 'ef thee doesn't sign the teetotum, I'll be tha death av tha, iss I will.'

I felt all oogly like, but I dedn want to be killed twice ovver, an' so I 'greed to sign un, an' sign un I ded. I found out arterwards that I wodn' dead 'toal, an' that they awnly maade out I was dead to frighten me, an' borrowed the coffin – a second hand waun, that dedn' fit somebody – from the carpenter's shop.

I signed tha teetotum, for I thoft to myself what a wisht job 'twould ha bin ef 'twas all true, an' I had railly waaked up to find meself dead! An' arter he was signed I thoft, well now I got un I may as well keep un, an' I've got un home wropped up en a yalla pocket hankercher sticked in my high poller hat in the corner of the long drawer of Granny's chist of drawers, in our best bedroom, to this very day.

Betsy Jaane hasn't a-got ovver the best taypot yet, an' she caan't clunkey from her Granny's cups an' saucers, but she's comin' round a bit, and so I'm hoppin' that next 'eear, when Faisten Time do come agaain, my deventures will be more pleasanter to spaik 'bout.

Betsy Jaane es fittin' a bit of turmut stew for supper, me dears, so I must coil up me ropes in the jawin' line, or Betsy Jaane will be wanting to lay the clooas line 'bout my back, or to oil my eear weth the turmut stew, for though she's a dear good cratur, she've got a bit of a temper, and doan't like the turmut stew burnt fast to the bottom of the crock. Aw, what lovely turmut stew she do maake! Aw, lovely sure 'nough! I would ax ee in my dears, but I doan't know what Betsy Jaane's 'pinion es 'bout it.

The Taaty Paasty

Morgan Anthony

Now tuch your pipe, comraades, says I,
And niver be too haasty,
And I will make a fooch to rhyme
About the taaty-paasty.

There's mait enuf of iv'ry soort,
All fillin' like and taasty;
But for a Carnish miner's mait,
Give me a taaty-paasty!

Good Lor'! – What lots of em I've carr'd
To bal when I were little –
Baaked 'pon the brandis long weth furse,
En baaker and en kittle!

Iss, slabs es haandy, I deer say –
There's piles o' new things maaken –
But give me Mawther's baaker, soas!
That's theer the theng for baaken!

Slabs, kitcheners, and what besides –
I'd fooch awaay them traade.
No paasties iver was so good
As them that Mawther maade!

Seems now I see her clutten down,
The fire 'ook in her haand,
A-foochen 'bout the burnen sticks,
And doin' paasties graand!

An' then she'd saay, 'They're ready, bleeve!'
Jist as the fit wud taake her,
An' slip a knife right in between
The bake-ire and the baaker.

'Aw, they're done beautiful!' she'd saay,
'Frawl wan es burnt a bit –
Well, niver mind, 'tes luck, I s'pos:
We taake what we can git!'

'Now maaidens, taake they paasties up,
An' put en all you've got!
A pass'l o' hungry grawen booys
Well ait a braa' big lot!'

Et may not be sa very rech,
Nor yit sa very shawy,
But nawthen's like a paasty, soas,
To feed a grawen booy!

An' then, they aren't like pie or stew,
Or brath, or fish-an'-tates,
Or fried petates; for they you must
Have baasins, dishes, plates.

An' knives and farks, an' spoons an' things,
An' taable to be sure;
But for a paasty hands an' jaws
Will do, weth nawthen moore.

Jist drap'n en your handkercher.
Wan carner sticken out;
Then bit and chow which way you mind,
You're right enough, no doubt.

You needn't have et en no room,
Nor set upon no cheer;
Joist chose a splat of handy grass
An' setty down right theer.

Or lean your back agin a hedge,
Or quatty 'pon a booard,
An' then you wudn', ef you cud,
Chaange denners weth a loord!

So good luck to the paasty, booys,
The aiter and the maaker:
And good luck to the baaken-ire,
The brandis and the baaker –

Good luck to all the Carnish booys,
That niver yit was baiten;
A paasty may they niver want,
Nor stummick for to ait'n!

Manuring the St Agnes Church Tower

As for that theere story they goat 'bout us, that we dunged our tower to maake un grow, 'twas nawthin moore than this: 'I'll have ivy graw oal roun' the tower,' says the passon. 'And so you shall, my dear,' says the church warden.

And when the passon was gone, he beginned to put some in. A Trura man looked in and seed un, and thoft he was dungin' the tower to maake un graw, and went hum and said so: and from that time they do axe how the tower do git on. And that's how it was, and nawthin' moore. And the ivy never grawd, nor the tower of coose; and the moore the pity, for he's oncommon short, but we're goin' to have a new waun.

[The tower of St Agnes parish church was rebuilt in 1840.]

A Chrestmas play

I were oop to cozen Nic Carnoweth's laast New Year's Eve, and ef so be thee do wesh, thee shust knaw the whole coose of et. We'd a fine denar sure enough; a few broth, a couple of as nice ploffy yung mabjers as one wed wesh to put a knife en, a starry-gazey pie, and a thoomping figgy pudden; and aafter that a little coostom.

And so we discoosed away quite comfortable like about the Chrestmas stock oontell the evenen when some more neybors comed among us soon after teening time, and we was a braave coompany; and then us had soome heavy cake and scaal cream and fogans. Well, then we was well glut, and we'd a nigh cracked our craws we thoft we wed have some make-games and sich like, but afore we cu'd git no further in thickey theer notions, there comed en a grinning gaukum, and tould us as how a giz-daunce was to door with the auntient play of St George, so, as I never had seen sich condudles afore, I gived my censure for they, thof cozen Nic wed have strove me down agen them, but we lev'd he alone and dedn't mind un.

So in they come, and we made hoam the door to stop out any of the straange chaps who was a scrounging en; and then the shaw begin'd en a jeffy. There was ould Feyther Chrestmas, a funny ould codger, with a make-wise feace possed on top of his aun, and es long white wig, trapesing about and getting en es tantrums, like for to make thee splet tha sides; and there were the doctor as they caal'd un with a three-corner piked hat, and es feace all rudded and whited, with spurticles on top of es nawse.

And there was one en a maiden's bed-gound and coats with ribands, and a nackin en es hand and a gowk, and the other yungsters was en white weth ribands tied all upon their shirt sleeves with nackins and swords and sich caps as I never seed. They was half a fathom high made of pastyboord, weth powers of beads and loaking glass, and other noshions, and shrids of ould cloth stringed 'pon slivers of pith hanging down – so, they strutted about so braave and rumbustious as lubber-cocks.

And then they gived the word to begin, and ould Feyther Christmas stepped out and said –

Here come I, ould Feyther Chrestmas,
Welcome or welcome not,
I do hope ould Feyther Chrestmas
Will never be forgot.
I am not a comed here, for to laugh or to jeer,
But for a pocketful of money, and a skin-full of beer;

Ef you well not beleeve what I do say,
Come en the bould Toorkish Knight – clear the way.

The ould gaffer then scrambled oop and down the room, shawing a curius figur, and when he'd tarvied about so as to make enough sport, in comed the Toorkish Knight, and said:

Here comes I, a Toorkish Knight,
Comed from the Toorkish land to fight;
And ef Saint George do meet me here,
I'll try es courage wethout fear.

Then a yungster come out very forthly,

Here come I, St George!

Anan! says I, none of thy doodling, thee bean't St George, no more than me; as ef I dedn't knaw thee wast Jan Trelubbas down to Nancegibbie croft. St George aketha! Why I do knaw all the havage of thee, thee crazed hoddymandoddy, for all tha braave cloase.

Hoosh! say my cozen, what's the odds, dont'ee knaw 'tes aunly play-acting like, making wise as a body might say. Auh! says I to he, that's of et es et, well lev he be St George then in coose; so away to go agen:

> Here comes I, St George,
> That worthy champion bould,
> And weth my swoord and spear,
> I winn'd three crowns of gould.
> I fout the dragon bould,
> And broft en to the slaughter,
> By that I gained fair Sabra,
> The King of Egypt's daughter.

Then the Toorkish knight stepped up to he, and said,

> St George, I pray be not too bould,
> Ef thy blood be hot, I'll soon make et could.

And St George ded answer he

> Thou Toorkish Knight I pray forbear,
> I'll make thee dread my swoord and spear.

Then they goes to fight, and tears away like the Stampses, and the Toorkish Knight do fall upon the planchen, and do try to get up, but St George do stank upon em and wain't lev him to, when he do seem afeard and do say,

> Oh pardon me, St George, oh pardon me I crave,
> Oh pardon me thes once, and I well be thy slave.

St George do answer

> I'll never pardon a Toorkish Knight,
> Therefore arise and try thy might.

Then he do immedjantly get up, and away they cuts life for life, untell the Knight do receive sich a whap, that he do fall dead. St George ded cry out as ef mazed,

> Es there a doctor to be found
> To cure a deep and deadly wound?

And the doctor comed forward as ef to pomster the dead Toork.

> Auh! yes there es a doctor to be found,
> To cure a deep and deadly wound!
> 'What can 'ee cure?' says ould Feyther Chrestmas.
> All sorts of diseases,
> Whatever thee pleases;
> The itch, the palsy and the gout,
> Ef the deuce es en him,
> I'll pull en out.

And what is thy fee?
Fefteen pound et es my fee,
The money to lay down;
But as 'tes sich a roag as he,
I'll cure en for ten pound.
I do carr' a little bottle of alicumpane.
Here Jack, take a little of my flip-flap,
Pour et down thy tip-top,
Rise up and fight agen.

So the doctor ded cure he, and away to fight agen, but St George were too much for he, and kill'd un as dead as a saalt pilcher and ded cry,

Here come I, St George, from Britain I ded spring,
I'll fight the Dragon bould, my wonders to begin,
I'll clip es wings that he shan't fly,
I'll cut un down or else I die.

Then forth comed the Dragon:

Who es he that do seek the Dragon's bloud,
And do call so angry and so loud?
That English dog, well he before me stand?
I'll cut en down weyth my bould hand,
Weth my long teeth and scurvy jaw,
I'll seize un up wethin my maw.
Of sich I'd break up hafe a score,
And stay my stomach, tell I'd more.

Then they fights, tell the Dragon es thraw'd, and the Doctor do come agen, and they discoos as they ded afore, and joist after I seed one step out, as they caal'd the King of Egypt's daughter, but I knaw'd he, so I said, 'Nan! nan! I caan't lev this quiet, I am better speak please sure, it ain't fitty to have sich strams, I am better not hould my tongue no longer. What! call he a maiden, why I do knaw he for a buddle boy up along to bal.' – 'Now do'ee be quiet, Sose,' says cozen Nic, 'titch pipe a few, why I tell'ee he be aunly a maiden for the nonce, do'ee be quiet thee assneger, or thee'st be turned to doors.'

Auh! well, says I, a fine passel of toatledum patticks they be sure nough, lev them make heaste on – and St George said,

Gentlemen and ladies, the sport is almost ended,
Come pay to the box, et es highly commended.
The box et wud speak, ef et had a but a tongue,
Come thraw en your money and thenk et no wrong.

So we giv'd them some cuyn 'caase they shudn't go away leary, and they singed a song weth a daance, and off they trampses, and us to our geames again.

At supper, we'd got a squab pie and mashes of 'taties and pilchers, and then some curll singing, and finished weth Tom Toddy, where one do take oop es cup of licker, and do put ento et a piece of candle lighted, and his comraades do sing,

Tom Toddy es come hoam, come hoam,
Tom Toddy es come hoam,
Weth es eyes burnt, and es nawse burnt,
And es eyelids burnt also.
Tom Toddy es come hoam, come hoam,
Tom Toddy es come hoam.

And he do try and drenk up es licker en the mean time and depend on't 'tes pure sport to see how the candle do flop agen es feace, and nawse, as et be so kicklish; and et made me quite timersome, and I thoft I shu'd had clunkt candle and all when it comed to me, and were en a cruel taking. Well, then we said good night'ee, and when we got to door we thoft there had ben lashes of rain, but it were but a skew; howsobe et maade the roaad all sloshy and slottery, and as my coorse were up Clodgy Laane, I were en a pretty shaape when I fetched hoam; and were glad to put ma head 'pon the pellowe bere, 'ees I were: but I've ben a bit hoozy sence.

And Aunt Betty had a ben too forthey en teeming out her licker, and p'raps were a little boosy, and she were found 'pon the sea shoare, laid down as ef she were to bed, and the water were comed oop to her feace and flopping agen et, and she were a saying quite genteely like, 'Nat a drap more, nat a drap more, thankee.'

Glossary

alicumpane	elecampane, a healing herb	night coor	night shift
bal	mine	oogly	ugly, cross
bewattled	rattled, shaken up, bewitched	perfessor	professed Methodist
blaw	blow, breathe	planchen	floorboards
box heater	part of a smoothing iron	pomster	administer medicine to pane
brandis	trivet	quarry scat	a blow
charley	Charles I style beard	scat in	smashed shoot it
cloam(in)	pottery	shut to un skew	shower
coose	course	slab	kitchen stove
coosing	chasing	soas	friend, mate
clukey	squat	skrooch	crutch
clunk(y)	swallow	splatty	marked with 'splashes'
crowe	yard		
dandy-dogs	hell-hounds	St Anns	St Agnes
drash	throw	stagged	muddy
faist	feast	stamps	ore-pounding machinery
fang	take, collect		
fire inyun	steam engine	strik	move
fooch	force, try,	stuggy	stocky
forthey	forward	tarvy	caper
fuss	furze	teem	empty a vessel
fust long	firstly	teening	lighting-up
gowk	bonnet	timberen hill	staircase
grezzle	laugh	touch-pipe	break for a smoke
gaukum	fool, clown		
hoddymandoddy	simpleton	to-waunce	at once
hoozy	hoarse	town place	farmyard
keeve	large tub	towse	disorder
kiddlywink	ale-house	trade	stuff, substance
leck and jowds	smithereens	whem	whim, or winding engine
lurgy	disease causing exhaustion	wisht	melancholy, eerie, or supernatural
maazed	confused, bewildered, crazy		
mabjer	pullet	yaffer	heifer
mellerd	miller	zound	faint, swoon
missment	mistake		